RESTART CLARINET

Written by Christopher Walters

ISBN: 978-1-84938-973-0

Visit Hal Leonard Online at
www.halleonard.com

Contact us:
Hal Leonard
7777 West Bluemound Road
Milwaukee, WI 53213
Email: info@halleonard.com

In Europe, contact:
Hal Leonard Europe Limited
42 Wigmore Street
Marylebone, London, W1U 2RY
Email: info@halleonardeurope.com

In Australia, contact:
Hal Leonard Australia Pty. Ltd.
4 Lentara Court
Cheltenham, Victoria, 3192 Australia
Email: info@halleonard.com.au

Order No. AM1002826

Author: Christopher Walters.
Project editor: Lizzie Moore.
Book design: Camden Music.
Photography: Matthew Ward.
Clarinet played by Christopher Walters.
CD mixed and mastered by Jonas Persson.
Cover design by Tim Field.
Cover photograph courtesy of Robert Kneschke - Fotolia.

Printed in the EU.

About the author:
Christopher Walters is a professional clarinettist, teacher and writer.
He has taught in schools around London, privately and at the Kenya Conservatoire of Music,
and has performed as a member of various orchestras, ensembles and West End show bands.
He has written for several magazines and websites, and is currently editor of *Music Teacher*
magazine.

This book is dedicated to Dame Thea King, 1925-2007, in memory of many happy lessons.

Introduction

If you used to play the clarinet and would now like to play it again, you've come to the right place. This book contains all the information you will need to make a flying restart, including 12 fantastic tunes, each with its own set of manageable practice goals, and a fabulous CD of backing tracks and complete demonstrations. With this book you'll find getting back into the groove easier and more enjoyable than you could ever have imagined.

So, without further ado, let's get on with the task in hand.

First things first

Before you start playing again there are a few important preparations and safety checks that you'll need to make. These will save you time later on and ensure that you enjoy playing the clarinet as much as possible.

First, your equipment. Has your clarinet been sitting in a cupboard for years? If so, it would be a good idea to take it down to your local music shop, where someone experienced will be able to confirm that it's all in working order. While you're there, buy yourself some new reeds. Reeds that are years old may look OK, but they will probably be long past their best in terms of sound and playability. So treat yourself to some new ones that will allow you to sound as good as you really are—and go for a softer strength if you are in any doubt.

Perhaps you didn't keep your first clarinet and need a new one. If so, a reputable retailer should be your first port of call, as car boot sales and eBay are not always reliable options. The leading clarinet manufacturers all make excellent plastic or beginner models, so don't feel the need to buy the clarinet equivalent of a Porsche—you can always upgrade later on. Second-hand instruments can offer real value but vary hugely in terms of quality, so be careful if you are considering this route and take advice where possible.

With your equipment sorted, it's on to safety check number two—you. Whether you prefer to play standing up or sitting down, make sure you put your music stand at a height that will allow you to hold your head in a natural, relaxed position. If you prefer to play sitting down, use a flat chair that will not encourage you to slouch and will allow you to put both feet flat on the ground. Simple steps like these are an effective way to avoid muscle tension and are well worth devoting a few moments to at the start of each practice session.

You are now ready to do some playing! But before we launch into our pieces, let's make sure you can remember the basics.

Remembering the basics

As you've played the clarinet before you'll probably remember how to put it together, but in case you're in any doubt, the diagram on page 57 shows you the correct alignment of the clarinet.

Remember to apply cork grease to any stiff joints and to moisten the reed by popping it into your mouth as you assemble the rest of the instrument. Once moistened, be careful to align the reed correctly with the sides and tip of the mouthpiece, as small variations here can affect the response of the whole instrument and can sometimes cause squeaks.

The photo opposite shows a good example of how to align the reed.

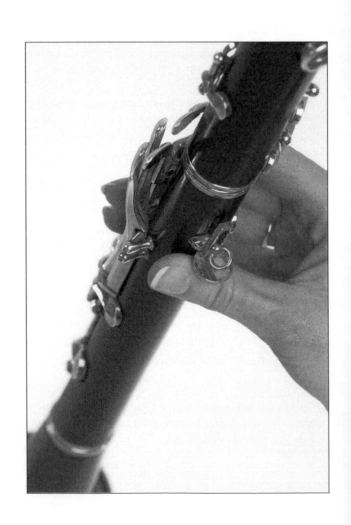

You'll remember that your right hand goes at the bottom of the instrument, with your thumb underneath the thumb rest, which should sit roughly on the joint of your thumb nearest the tip.

Your right-hand thumb position is important because much of the weight of the instrument is carried here. If your clarinet has an adjustable thumb rest, experiment with different positions until you find the one that feels most comfortable.

Remember the word **embouchure**? It means mouth position, and restarting the clarinet after a break is the perfect opportunity to check you have it just right.

Simply, your top teeth should sit on the top of the mouthpiece and your lower lip should cushion the reed at the bottom. This means that a bit of your lower lip will cover your lower teeth, but not too much—when the clarinet is in your mouth, some of your lower lip should still be visible on the outside.

Finally, your lips should seal around the mouthpiece with a slight smile at the corners. The photo opposite is a good guide.

Inhale deeply through your mouth and try playing a note. How did it sound? If you are struggling to make a sound, keep trying—there's a knack to it, and it's sure to come flooding back soon enough.

If problems persist, experiment with the amount of mouthpiece you are putting into your mouth. Too much, and you risk squeaking or sounding honky; too little and it's hard to make a sound at all.

Also, check the angle at which you are holding the clarinet. There's room for a bit of variation here, but something like 45 degrees (i.e., not right next to your body or straight out like a trumpet) will help you form the securest embouchure.

A note about the accompanying CD

The CD is designed to make your experience of restarting the clarinet even easier by giving you an audio demonstration of all the pieces in this book. But when you first start learning the pieces, it's a good idea to work at a slower tempo until all your notes are secure, however, only up to full performance tempo when you are ready. It's also a good idea to wait until you are fairly comfortable with each piece before attempting to play along with the backing tracks.

TIP

Buy a **metronome**. This simple device will keep a steady beat so you don't have to! For slow practice it can be a great help, and you can increase the tempo by the smallest amount until you reach a comfortable performance speed.

Should I get a teacher?

Whether or not you need a teacher is a question that only you can answer. If you can remember a lot about playing the clarinet and just want to enjoy playing the pieces in this book, you may not need a teacher. But if you feel that you need a bit more help than a refresher course like this can provide, then perhaps you do.

If you decide that you do need one, be sure to discuss with them exactly what you want to achieve before you start your lessons. The great thing about restarting as an adult is that you can drive your own learning. It's your decision—whether you want to go in for exams or just have fun.

With or without a teacher, it's unlikely that this book alone will be enough to support you in learning. As you work through these pages, you might find that you'd like to explore certain kinds of music in greater depth, in which case you should investigate the **Guest Spot** series of books, each of which also comes with a playalong CD.

The many *Guest Spot* books include the following titles:

- Classical Favourites (AM984456)
- 20 Jazz Greats (AM970453)
- Showstoppers (AM941820)
- Ballads (AM941787)
- Classic Blues (AM941743)
- The Beatles (NO90682)
- Abba (AM960905)
- Film Themes (AM941864)
- Sixties Hits (AM988702)
- Seventies Hits (AM989219)
- Eighties Hits (AM991034)
- Nineties Hits (AM952853)

Another series you should try is *Playalong With A Live Band*. This is similar to *Guest Spot*, but with backing tracks recorded live.

In this series you will find:

- Swing (AM997568)
- Blues (AM991958)
- Gospel (AM997678)
- Soul (AM991914)
- Latin (AM997623)
- Jazz (AM991870)

If you'd like more help with the basics, check out *Absolute Beginners Clarinet* (AM1002430). For more help with theory and notation, try *How To Read Music* (AM91452) and *How To Crack Music Theory* (AM991716). All these books are published by Music Sales and are available from your local music shop or online from **www.musicroom.com**.

Now, on to our first piece!

Ode To Joy (for counting and tonguing)

'Ode To Joy' is a much-loved melody taken from the final movement of Beethoven's ninth symphony. It's also a great piece for reminding yourself about two important parts of playing the clarinet: *counting* and *tonguing.*

Counting

At the beginning of the music, after the **treble clef** (𝄞) and the two **sharp** signs (♯), you'll notice a **C** sign. The **C** sign tells you that there are four **crotchets** in a **bar**, and that each of these crotchets equals one **beat**. This is the most common rhythmic foundation in all music. The **C** actually stands for **common time**.

To play this piece rhythmically, you will need to have a firm idea of how fast you would like to play it (if you use the backing track then this will be decided for you, but it's a good idea to practise without it first). Before you play, imagine what the music will sound like and begin to tap out a beat with your hand or foot, or in your head. The word **allegro**, written above the music, is Italian for 'lively', but it might be an idea to settle on a slower tempo for comfortable practice.

> ### FACT
>
> **Beat** (or **pulse**) means the underlying heartbeat of the music—what you would tap your foot to.
>
> **Rhythm** means something different: it is the various patterns of long and short notes that make up the melody. In 'Ode To Joy', the *rhythm* follows the beat quite closely and they are often the same.

Once you have a feel for the beat, count one bar of "one, two, three, four" in your head and then start to play the piece. When you come to play with the backing track you will need to count four lots of "one, two, three, four" i.e., four bars, before you start to play. Listen to the performance track to help with any rhythms that look confusing. Remember that two notes of the same pitch that are linked by a curved line (as in bars 16–17) are **tied**; this means that you need to add their values together to produce one longer note.

Tonguing

Unless notes are joined together with a **slur** (a curved line connecting notes of different pitches, as in bars 14 and 15), you need to *tongue* them. The analogy here is with speech. Imagine speaking without the first consonant of every word—that's what the clarinet played without tonguing can sound like! Fortunately, instead of a whole range of different consonants, the clarinet has just one: 't'. So when you play a note on the clarinet, you need to give it a 't' at the beginning. Do this by placing your tongue on the reed before you blow. Then, as you start to blow, take your tongue off the reed to produce a crisp 't' sound at the start of the note. This usually works best with the tip of your tongue on the tip of the reed, but everyone is different, so do what sounds best for you.

REMEMBER

The two **sharp** signs at the beginning of the piece are positioned at F and C, which tells you that all the Fs and Cs in this piece are sharps. If you need reminding of the fingerings for these or any other notes, check the fingering chart on pages 57–59.

TIP

This piece is in two sections, with the same tune repeated an octave higher in the second section (from bar 33). For a more manageable challenge, play the first section and then stop!

Ode To Joy

Music by Ludwig Van Beethoven

Allegro

Jupiter (for more counting and stamina)

'Jupiter,' from the popular *Planets* suite by Holst, is our next piece.

Counting

There is no **C** at the beginning of this piece. In its place you will notice $\frac{3}{4}$, which means there are just three crotchet beats per bar instead of four, another very common rhythmic foundation. The **C** and $\frac{3}{4}$ signs are both examples of **time signatures**, which appear at the start of music to give you important information about how to count the piece.

Before you play 'Jupiter', get the feel of the tempo by counting bars of 'one, two, three' in your head. Instead of **allegro** (lively), this piece is marked **andante maestoso**, which tells you to play at a moderate walking pace (*andante*) and majestically (*maestoso*). You will therefore need a slower tempo for 'Jupiter' than you used for 'Ode To Joy'.

Stamina

Stamina is an important consideration for clarinet players. 'Jupiter' requires a lot of stamina because it is relatively long, relatively loud and played at a fairly slow tempo. The louder and slower you play, the more air you need—which requires more stamina.

The way to conserve your stamina is by controlling your breathing. In this piece, breathe only where you see this symbol: ✓.

Inhale deeply through your mouth and fill your lungs, and aim to expel all the air in your lungs before you take your next breath. Try to ensure that your 'in' and 'out' breaths are well matched—if you run out of air before the next ✓ sign, breathe more deeply; if you still have unused air at the next ✓ sign, inhale slightly less.

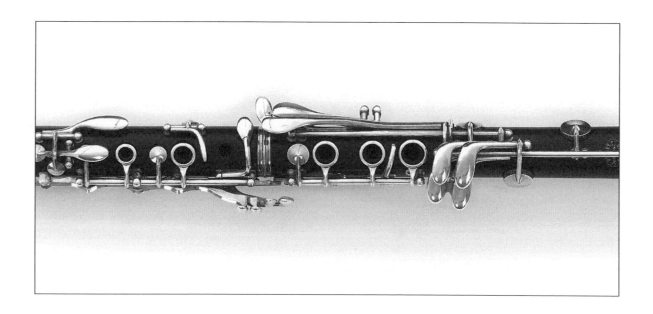

Jupiter

Music by Gustav Holst

Andante maestoso

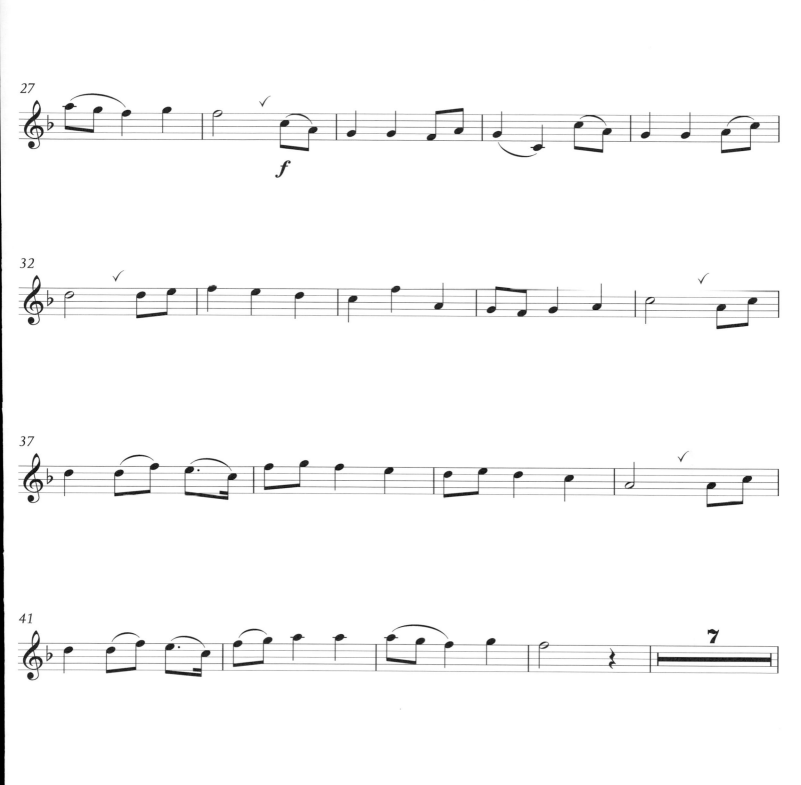

rall.

Amazing Grace (for low notes and crossing the break)

Next we tackle the classic spiritual 'Amazing Grace'.

p cantabile

Low notes

This piece begins on low E, the clarinet's lowest note, played softly. You will need to ensure that your fingers cover the holes very precisely—check the fingering chart on pages 57–59 if you need help remembering the fingering. The low F♯ in bar 7 will require similar care.

> **TIP**
>
> Practise low E and F♯ on their own, holding them as long as you can, to check that your fingers are covering the holes correctly. Combine this with breath-control practice by starting each note ***p***, getting louder to reach ***f***, and then dying away again to return to ***p***.
>
> The musical word for getting louder is **crescendo** and the word for getting softer is **diminuendo**. Crescendo and diminuendo are represented by these symbols ——————— which you will see in bars 27 and 29 of 'Amazing Grace'.

Crossing the break

Crossing the break means moving between the **lower** and **middle registers** of the clarinet, which can be tricky because it involves changing many fingers just to move between two notes that are right next to each other. Control and precision are therefore required!

On the clarinet, the break lies between B♭ and B. This excerpt from 'Amazing Grace' includes three break crossings in just two bars (the example above): from A to C♯; from B to A; and from A to C♯.

If you've been practising your long notes on low E and F♯ you'll already be an expert at B and C♯ above the break, because E is the same fingering as B, and F♯ is the same as C♯—with the addition of the **register key** in both cases. Be even more careful as you practise these notes—notes above the break require especially precise finger placement.

Once you are secure with B and C♯ above the break, try moving slowly and smoothly between A and B, and then back to A. Don't tongue these notes; just play them all in one breath and concentrate on smoothness. Listen carefully—if it sounds good, you are doing it right. Once you have mastered A-B-A, move on to A-C♯-A. Then, when you are ready, practise the short excerpt from 'Amazing Grace' above. Soon you'll be ready to tackle the whole piece.

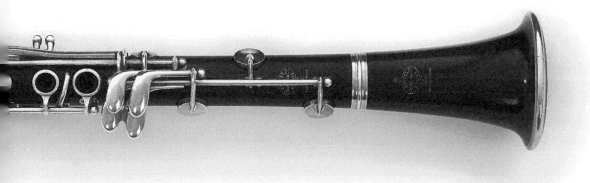

Amazing Grace

Words & Music by John Newton

Moon River
(for legato playing and sounding good in the upper-middle register)

Next we have a film classic loved by *Breakfast At Tiffany's* fans everywhere—'Moon River'.

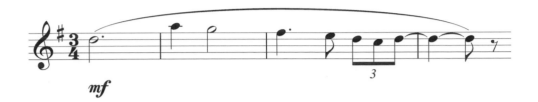

Legato

Legato means smooth playing, and is marked on the music with a **slur** (a long curved line). All the notes under a slur are to be played smoothly. This means that the only time you need to tongue in the passage above is at the very beginning, to give the first note a crisp start. After that, you should blow as if you were blowing one very long note—except that you move your fingers, of course. Listen to the performance track for a demonstration.

Sounding good in the upper-middle register

The clarinet's high notes can be quite powerful—but in this piece you need to make a lyrical, sweet sound on your high notes. Think of it as 'taming' your high notes! In order to do this, you need to use something called **support**.

TIP

Support is a way to achieve fine control over the air you blow into the clarinet. Simply, it is the act of holding back air so that it doesn't all rush out of your lungs at once.

To achieve support, inhale deeply through your mouth, then push out firmly with your abdominal muscles, expanding your belly as if you were trying to hold up a pair of baggy trousers. Hold this tension right through your exhalation until the very end of your breath.

Not only should this make your high notes easier to control, it should also make your breath last longer.

Support is the most effective way to control your high notes, but some players find that a little extra firmness in the embouchure can also help. Other players find making an 'ee' vowel shape inside the mouth helpful.

Have fun experimenting with these techniques—and remember to be patient!

REMEMBER

When 'taming' your high notes, you are listening out for two things: *tone quality* and *tuning* (or *intonation*).

High notes tend to dip in pitch, so listen carefully to the sound you are making and experiment with the methods above to achieve the securest tuning you can manage. You may want to invest in an electronic tuner—or a smart phone tuning app—to help confirm that you are playing in tune.

See theory page 60 to work out the structure of this piece.

Moon River

Words by Johnny Mercer & Music by Henry Mancini

The Girl From Ipanema
(for syncopation and good throat notes)

Next we move on to a bossa nova classic—'The Girl From Ipanema'.

Syncopation

Syncopation (rhythm that features off-beats, usually found in jazz and popular music) often looks complicated written down, but is usually intuitive and natural to play. Therein lies the most common problem with syncopation—interpreting it from the notation.

> ### TIP
>
> The way to process syncopation, and indeed all complex rhythm, is by a technique called *subdivision*. This involves counting using the smallest rhythmic unit found in the syncopation—in this case a *quaver* (half a beat).
>
> The excerpt above shows the first four bars of the melody from 'The Girl From Ipanema', with the beats divided into quavers, written above the notes. You can see that the first note is worth three quavers, the second, one quaver and so on.

Once you have counted the rhythm of the excerpt above using the subdivision technique, play it, taking as much care over the rhythm as when you were just counting. Play it a few more times—you should start to relax into the syncopation without having to think so much about the counting. When you come to tackle the complete piece, you may choose to write in the quaver subdivisions from start to finish.

Good throat notes

Throat notes are the notes just below the break: B♭, A, G♯ and G. Most of the holes on the clarinet are open for these notes; consequently they can have a thin tone if not properly looked after.

Look at 'The Girl From Ipanema' from bar 25 onwards. Each short phrase begins with a sustained throat note: first a G♯ and then an A. Practise long notes on these pitches. How do they sound? **Support** will help them sound better—try supporting gently and see what difference it makes. Allow time for the difference to show—as always, patience is everything. You can also improve the resonance of throat notes by depressing any of the fingers of your right hand. Experiment carefully with this technique, making sure that it doesn't compromise your tuning.

The Girl From Ipanema

Music by Antonio Carlos Jobim. English Words by Norman Gimbel. Original Words by Vinicius De Moraes.

Pieces for enjoyment

Congratulations on completing the first five pieces! Hopefully they have helped you remember some old techniques, as well as introducing you to a few new ones. Now it's time to leave you to your own devices with the following seven pieces:

Yesterday This timeless Beatles anthem will help you develop your expressive playing. Imagine the words as you play for maximum expressive impact.

I Say A Little Prayer There's plenty of syncopation in this Burt Bacharach classic, so be sure to subdivide throughout. Watch out for the changing time signatures too—but remember that the beat always stays the same.

Bridge Over Troubled Water This Simon & Garfunkel favourite is another test of stamina. Be careful to save some energy for the climax at the very end of the piece. Listen to the demonstration on the CD to hear how the 'late gliss.' should sound in bars 15–16 and 43–44.

Fever With its sparse accompaniment, 'Fever' gives you a chance to develop your quiet playing—with the occasional loud outburst! Try to capture the smoky sounds of jazz.

Mrs Robinson The complexity of the syncopation is taken up a notch in this second Simon & Garfunkel tune. Keep subdividing, and try to communicate the lively energy of the music.

Good Vibrations This Beach Boys hit features swung quavers—listen to the demonstration track if you are unsure about how to perform these. This piece is another stamina challenge, moving through various keys—but well worth the effort!

When The Saints Go Marching In We end on a high with this Dixieland classic—perfectly suited to the clarinet. Although simple and well-known, the tune is presented here in a more complex and embellished form, similar to how a jazz clarinettist might interpret it. A final challenge for you to get your teeth into!

TIP

For many people, music is a social pastime. Now that you are becoming a more confident player, why not find out what music-making is going on in your area? 'Making Music', the umbrella body for amateur music-making, is a good place to start: **www.makingmusic.org.uk**.

REMEMBER

If you are unsure of any of the technical terms you encounter in any of the pieces, turn to the glossary on pages 51–54 of the book.

Yesterday

Words & Music by John Lennon & Paul McCartney

© Copyright 1965 Sony/ATV Music Publishing.

Gently

slower

dim.

I Say A Little Prayer

Words by Hal David & Music by Burt Bacharach

Bridge Over Troubled Water

Words & Music by Paul Simon

© Copyright 1969 Paul Simon (BMI).

late gliss.

poco cresc.

mf

3

8

Fever

Words & Music by John Davenport & Eddie Cooley

Relaxed swing

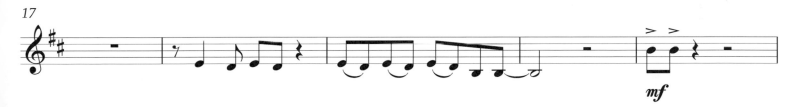

Mrs. Robinson

Words & Music by Paul Simon

With understated energy ♩ = 92

Good Vibrations

Words & Music by Brian Wilson & Mike Love

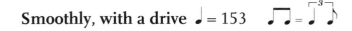

When The Saints Go Marching In

Traditional

50

Glossary

A tempo: back to original speed, usually after **rit.** or **rall.**

Accent (♩): a sharp attack at the beginning of the note

Al niente: to nothing, to silence, e.g., *dim. al niente*

Allegro: performance direction meaning 'lively'

Andante: performance direction, traditionally taken to mean 'moderate, walking pace'

Bar: unit of music, enclosed by barlines

Beat (or **pulse**): the regular underlying heartbeat of music

Break: division between registers

Cantabile: performance direction meaning 'play in a singing style'

Coda (⊕ **Coda**): final section of a piece

Common time or **four-four** (C or 𝟒/𝟒): four crotchet beats per bar

Cut common time or **two-two** (¢ or 𝟐/𝟐): two minim beats per bar

Crescendo or **cresc.** (⊂): instruction to get louder

Crotchet (♩): rhythmic value, most commonly worth one beat

Crotchet rest (𝄽): instruction to leave a one-beat gap

D.S. al Coda: instruction to continue playing from the 𝄋 sign, moving on to the **Coda** at the ⊕ sign

Diminuendo or **dim.** (⊃): instruction to get softer

Dotted crotchet (♩.): rhythmic value, most commonly worth one-and-a-half beats

Dotted minim (𝅗𝅥.): rhythmic value, most commonly worth three beats

Dotted quaver (♪.): rhythmic value, most commonly worth three-quarters of a beat

Dynamics: relates to the loudness and softness in music

Embouchure: mouth position when playing a wind instrument

Espressivo: performance direction meaning 'play expressively'

***f*:** dynamic marking, loud, stands for *forte*

Flat (♭): indicates that you should lower the pitch of a note by one semitone

Glissando: a rapid scale between two notes, often an embellishment

Grace note or **acciaccatura (♪):** a very quick note played before another note

Intonation: tuning

Legato: smooth, connected

Lower register: up to and including throat B♭

Maestoso: performance direction meaning 'play majestically'

Metronome: device that provides a steady beat and can be set at different tempos

Middle register: above B♮ on the middle line of the stave; up to and including C on two lines above the stave

Minim (♩): rhythmic value, most commonly worth two beats

Minim rest (▬): instruction to leave a two-beat gap

Molto: much, a lot

Multiple-bar rest (|——4——|): instruction to leave a gap for the amount of bars indicated

Natural (♮): cancels a flat or sharp

Non legato: not smooth

***mf*:** dynamic marking, fairly loud, stands for *mezzo forte*

***mp*:** dynamic marking, fairly soft, stands for *mezzo piano*

***p*:** dynamic marking, soft, stands for *piano*

Poco: a little

Poco a poco: little by little

Quaver (♪)**:** rhythmic value, most commonly worth half a beat

Quaver rest (𝄾)**:** instruction to leave a half-beat gap

Rall. (short for **rallentando):** performance direction meaning 'slow down'

Register: a particular part of the clarinet's range

Register key: pressed by the left-hand thumb, mostly used to change register

Rhythm: the patterns of various long and short notes that make up a melody

Rit. (short for **ritardando** or **ritenuto):** performance direction meaning 'slow down'

Semibreve (𝅝)**:** rhythmic value, most commonly worth four beats

Semibreve, or whole-bar, rest (𝄻)**:** instruction to leave a four-beat, or one-bar, gap

Semiquaver (𝅘𝅥𝅯)**:** rhythmic value, most commonly worth a quarter of a beat

Sharp (♯)**:** indicates that you should raise the pitch of a note by one semitone

Slur: curved line over two or more notes, indicating that you should connect the notes and play smoothly

Staccato (𝅘𝅥.)**:** detached

Subdivision: technique for understanding complex rhythm

Support: technique of controlling airstream by means of controlled tension of the diaphragm and abdominal muscles

Swing, swung quavers: jazzy rhythm in which quavers are played unevenly, with the first played longer than the second in each group of two

Syncopation: rhythm featuring off-beats, often found in jazzy and popular music

Tenuto (𝅘𝅥)**:** play the note's full value, perhaps with a little added emphasis

Three-four ($\frac{3}{4}$)**:** three crotchet beats per bar

Throat notes: notes just below the break

Tie: the rhythmic value of two notes added together, shown by a curved line joining two notes of the same pitch

Time signature: instruction at the start of music giving information on its rhythmic foundation

Tonguing: using the tongue to produce articulation

Treble clef (𝄞)**:** sign at the beginning of all clarinet music, also used for piano right hand, which indicates that you play in a treble, or high, range

Triplet: three notes of any rhythmic value to be played in the space of two, indicated by a number '3' over the notes

Theory Reminder

Accidentals (alter the pitch of notes)

♯   **Sharp:** raises the pitch of any note by a semitone

♭   **Flat:** lowers the pitch of any note by a semitone

♮   **Natural:** cancels out the effect of a sharp or flat

𝄪   **Double Sharp:** raises the pitch of any note by a whole tone

𝄫   **Double Flat:** lowers the pitch of any note by a whole tone

Note values

Semibreve: (whole note), or rest of equivalent length, lasts for four beats

Minim: (half note), or rest of equivalent length, lasts for two beats

Crotchet: (quarter note), or rest of equivalent length, lasts for a quarter of a semibreve and is commonly used as a one-beat note

Quaver: (eighth note), or rest of equivalent length, lasts for half a beat

Semiquaver: (sixteenth note), or rest of equivalent length, lasts for a quarter of a beat

Demisemiquaver: (thirty-second note), or rest of equivalent length, lasts for an eighth of a beat

Dot: increases the length of a note or rest by 50%

Tie: joins two notes together — the duration of the second is added to the first

Time signatures

Simple time

$\frac{2}{4}$ 2 crotchet beats in a bar

$\frac{3}{4}$ 3 crotchet beats in a bar

$\frac{4}{4}$ 4 crotchet beats in a bar

$\frac{3}{2}$ 3 minim beats in a bar

Compound time

$\frac{6}{8}$	6 quaver beats in a bar
$\frac{9}{8}$	9 quaver beats in a bar
$\frac{12}{8}$	12 quaver beats in a bar

Unusual time signatures

$\frac{5}{8}$	5 quaver beats in a bar
$\frac{7}{8}$	7 quaver beats in a bar
$\frac{11}{8}$	11 quaver beats in a bar

Other useful terms

Adagio: slow, between andante and largo

Allegretto: moderately fast

Cadenza: a solo section, often used to show off musical technique within a Concerto or similar piece

Concerto: a piece in three parts consisting of a soloist accompanied by an orchestra

Dolce: sweet/gentle

Grazioso: gracefully

Grave: slow and solemn

Largo: very slowly

Lento: slowly

Meno: less

Minuet: a piece originally from a dance in triple time

Moderato: moderately

Mosso: with movement

Movement: section of a large composition (e.g. 3rd movement of symphony no. 5)

Ostinato: a short pattern that is repeated

Overture: a piece used as an introduction to a dramatic, choral or instrumental composition

Più: more

Presto: very fast

Rondo: a musical form in which one section comes back time and time again

Rubato: a flexible tempo that can be pulled around to suit the style

Sonata: instrumental piece for piano, or solo instrument and piano, usually in three movements

Stringendo: pressing forward or moving on

Subito, sub.: suddenly

Symphony: a large composition for orchestra often in four movements

Tempo: the speed of a piece of music

Troppo: too much

Tutti: all, used to indicate where everyone plays together

Vibrato: repeated slight change in pitch to a single note to make a richer sound

Vivace: lively and fast

Clarinet Fingering Chart

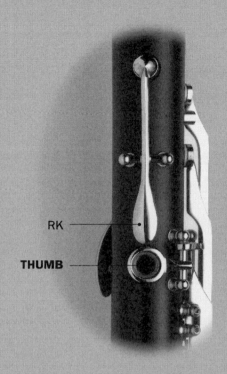

RK

THUMB

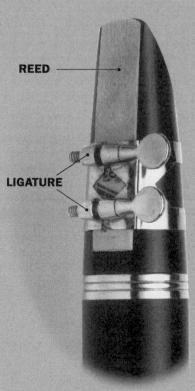

REED

LIGATURE

Mouthpiece

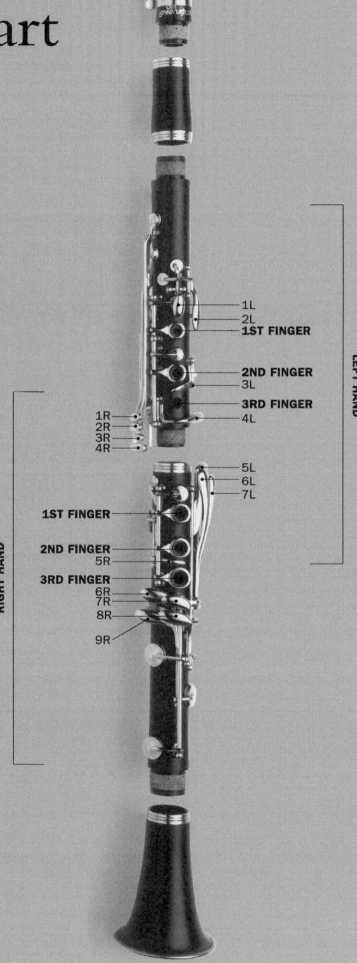

1L
2L
1ST FINGER

2ND FINGER
3L

3RD FINGER
4L

1R
2R
3R
4R

LEFT HAND

5L
6L
7L

1ST FINGER

2ND FINGER
5R

3RD FINGER
6R
7R
8R

9R

RIGHT HAND

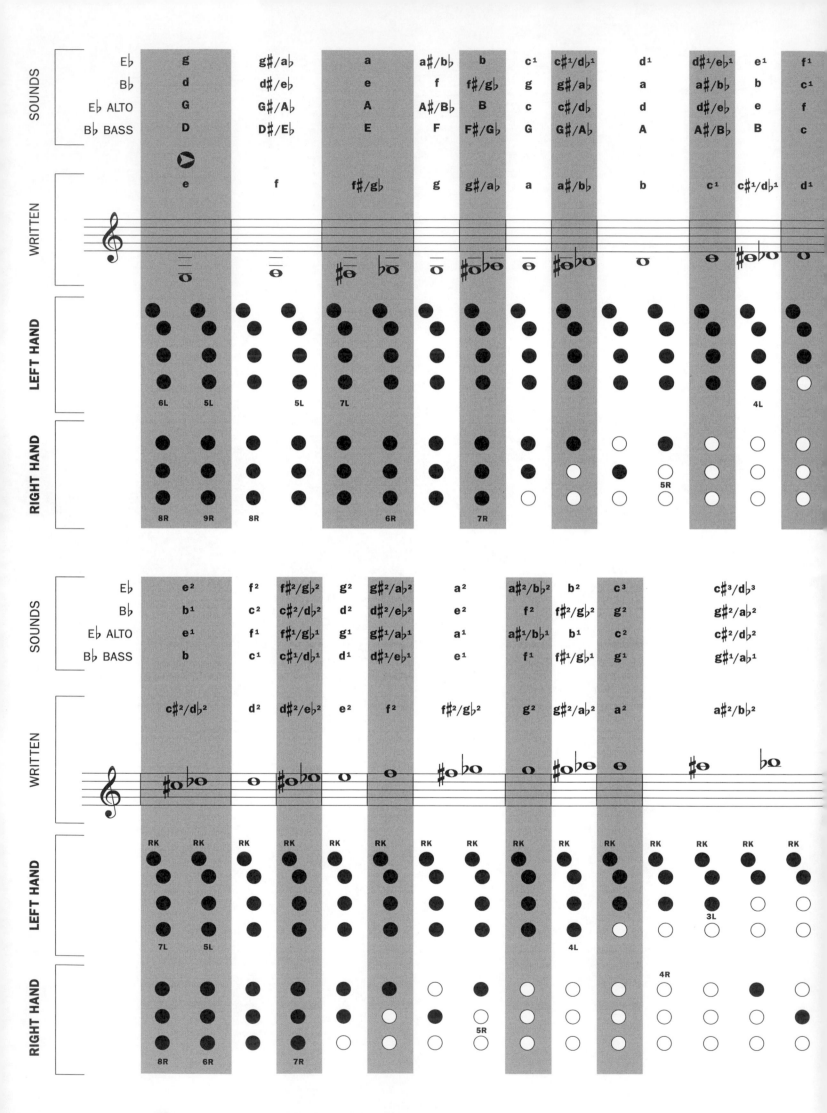

Indicates the lower limit of the best playing range for E♭, B♭, E♭ Alto and B♭ Bass Clarinets

Indicates the upper limit of the best playing range for E♭ and B♭ Clarinets   Indicates the upper limit of the best playing range for E♭ Alto and B♭ Bass Clarinets

Notation

Dotted Double Bars

:| Repeat what appears between the beginning of the piece and the dotted double bar.

|: :| Repeat what appears between the dotted double bars.

First and Second Endings

The first ending is played the first time through the passage; when the passage is repeated, the first ending is skipped and the second ending is played instead.

D.C. (Da Capo)

Return to the beginning of the piece.

D.C. al Fine

Return to the beginning and play to the indicated end (*Fine*). When playing a *D.C.* repeats are not taken and first endings are skipped.

D.S. (Dal Segno)

Return to the sign 𝄋

D.S. al Fine

Return to the sign 𝄋 and play to the indicated end (*Fine*).

D.S. al Coda

Play from the sign 𝄋 to the point at which ⊕ or *To Coda* appears; skip from there to the Coda. When playing a *D.%.* repeats are not taken and first endings are skipped.

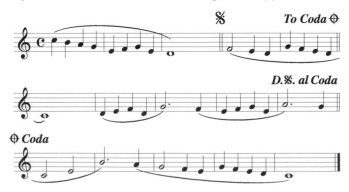

⊕ *Coda*

Repeat Signs

✗ Repeat the preceding measure.

Subdivision

ρ Subdivide the note value into the smaller values indicated by the slash(es).

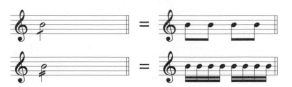

Two Instrument Parts on One Staff

Notes with stems *up* are played by the first player.

Notes with stems *down* are played by the second player.

The No. 1 indicates the first player, and the No. 2 the second player.

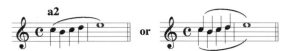

a2 (**a due**) indicates that both players play at once (in unison).

divisi indicates two separate parts written on the same staff.

Rests

Full-measure rests: the block hanging from the fourth line indicates a full-measure rest in all time signatures. (The No. 1 is sometimes added for clarity.)

Any rest shorter than a full measure is written according to the time signature.

Two-measure rests: in any time signature these may be written as enlarged full-measure rests and labelled with the No. 2. Rests longer than 2 measures use the ensemble rest sign.

Instrument Care

Things to have on hand
Soft absorbent cloth (for outside).
Weighted cloth swab (for inside).
Soft cloth (for mouthpiece).
Medium-bristle artist's paintbrush.
Cork grease or vaseline.
Key oil.
At least 1 extra reed.
Pencil with an eraser *(bring to every rehearsal)*.

Putting the instrument together
Since the clarinet's key mechanism crosses over the joints and could be easily twisted or bent, you should put it together and take it apart carefully. Use a little cork grease or vaseline on the corked joints. Then grasp the upper main section of the instrument so that the bridging mechanism is raised and, with a gentle twisting motion, slide the lower main section into position.

When the instrument is aligned properly, the pads cover the holes completely and you shouldn't have trouble with the notes in the lower register.

Cleaning
Wipe all the metal and wooden parts with a soft absorbent cloth after every use. Swab the inside of the instrument thoroughly after each use, even during intermissions, since the wood is very susceptible to rotting if not properly cared for. Use a weighted cloth, pulling it through the bore. Wash the mouthpiece frequently in warm soapy water, rinse it, and dry it with a soft cloth. An artist's paintbrush works well for cleaning around the keys and beneath the rods.

An occasional drop of oil on the screws, springs and moving parts will prevent rust and sticking keys, but be sure not to get any on the pads. Although you may apply a light coating of bore oil to the inside of the instrument yourself (avoiding getting any on the pads), this and other maintenance processes are best left to the repairman.

Storing
Before putting the instrument in its case, loosen the mouthpiece ligature to prevent warping. Remove the reed, rinse it, dry it, and store it on the flat surface of a reed holder.

Transposition

E♭ clarinet sounds a minor third above the written pitch. Rule: **Written C sounds E♭**

Written: Sounds:

B♭ clarinet sounds a major second below the written pitch. Rule: **Written C sounds B♭**

Written: Sounds:

E♭ alto clarinet sounds a major sixth below the written pitch. Rule: **Written C sounds E♭**

Written: Sounds:

B♭ bass clarinet sounds a major ninth below the written pitch. Rule: **Written C sounds B♭**

Written: Sounds:

Pitch System

The letter names which appear at the top of the fingering chart indicate the relative octave as well as the name of each pitch, as shown below.

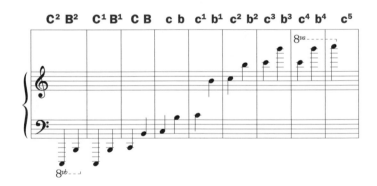

If you enjoyed this book you might like these other great publications

GUEST SPOT

PLAYALONG WITH A LIVE BAND

BLUES	JAZZ	SOUL
AM991958	AM991870	AM991914
GOSPEL	**LATIN**	**SWING**
AM997678	AM997623	AM997568

ABSOLUTE BEGINNERS CLARINET

AM1002430

RESTART CLARINET CD TRACK LISTING

FULL INSTRUMENTAL PERFORMANCES

1. ODE TO JOY
(BEETHOVEN)
DORSEY BROTHERS MUSIC LIMITED

2. JUPITER
(HOLST)
J. CURWEN & SONS LIMITED

3. AMAZING GRACE
(NEWTON)
DORSEY BROTHERS MUSIC LIMITED

4. MOON RIVER
(MERCER/MANCINI)
SONY/ATV HARMONY UK

5. THE GIRL FROM IPANEMA
(JOBIM/GIMBEL/DE MORAES)
UNIVERSAL MUSIC PUBLISHING LIMITED/
WINDSWEPT MUSIC (LONDON) LIMITED

6. YESTERDAY
(LENNON/McCARTNEY)
SONY/ATV MUSIC PUBLISHING (UK) LIMITED

7. I SAY A LITTLE PRAYER
(DAVID/BACHARACH)
UNIVERSAL/MCA MUSIC LIMITED/
WARNER/CHAPPELL MUSIC PUBLISHING LIMITED

8. BRIDGE OVER TROUBLED WATER
(SIMON)
UNIVERSAL/MCA MUSIC LIMITED

9. FEVER
(DAVENPORT/COOLEY)
LARK MUSIC LIMITED

10. MRS. ROBINSON
(SIMON)
UNIVERSAL/MCA MUSIC LIMITED

11. GOOD VIBRATIONS
(WILSON/LOVE)
UNIVERSAL MUSIC PUBLISHING LIMITED

12. WHEN THE SAINTS GO MARCHING IN
(TRADITIONAL)
DORSEY BROTHERS MUSIC LIMITED

BACKING TRACKS ONLY

13. ODE TO JOY
14. JUPITER
15. AMAZING GRACE
16. MOON RIVER
17. THE GIRL FROM IPANEMA
18. YESTERDAY
19. I SAY A LITTLE PRAYER
20. BRIDGE OVER TROUBLED WATER
21. FEVER
22. MRS. ROBINSON
23. GOOD VIBRATIONS
24. WHEN THE SAINTS GO MARCHING IN